Moments of
Faith

for Fathers

BARBOUR
PUBLISHING

Published by Barbour Publishing, Inc., P.O. Box 719, Uhrichsville, Ohio 44683, www.barbourbooks.com

Our mission is to publish and distribute inspirational products offering exceptional value and biblical encouragement to the masses.

Member of the
Evangelical Christian
Publishers Association

Printed in the United States of America.

Contents

Role Modeling

Wanted: Superheroes

I can do everything through him who gives me strength.
PHILIPPIANS 4:13 NIV

If Paul knew what he was talking about—and, of course, he did—the great apostle opened the door to people like us becoming superheroes. He saw the incredible possibilities of grace in our everyday lives.

Kids of Paul's day surely had their superheroes—those men of Old Testament times who stood head and shoulders above the crowd, whose exploits were held up as examples of strength, honor, and obedience. At bedtime, dads must have related the stories of what a child of God can do with a slingshot, the jawbone of a donkey, or even his bare hands. No Batmobiles or spider suits here. Enemies were overcome with God-given empowerment.

Today, fathers who understand the truth of Philippians 4:13 can be looked to as superheroes, as well. Our companionship, guidance, and example with our children can literally change their lives!

Father, please help me remember that some look to me for more than material benefits or good times. May my example change their lives.

Be such a person, and live such a life, that if every one were such as you, and every life such as yours, this earth would be God's paradise.

PHILLIPS BROOKS

Therefore be imitators of God as dear children. And walk in love, as Christ also has loved us and given Himself for us, an offering and a sacrifice to God for a sweet-smelling aroma.

EPHESIANS 5:1–2 NKJV

Nothing is so strong as gentleness, nothing so gentle as real strength.

FRANCIS DE SALES

Let your speech always be with grace, as though seasoned with salt, so that you will know how you should respond to each person.

COLOSSIANS 4:6 NASB

Daily duties are daily joys, because they are something which God gives us to offer unto Him, to do our very best, in acknowledgment of His love.

EDWARD BOUVERIE PUSEY

Every father is a hero in the eyes of his children.

UNKNOWN

Kind words produce their own image in men's
souls, and a beautiful image it is. They soothe
and quiet and comfort the hearer.

BLAISE PASCAL

You don't raise heroes; you raise sons.
And if you treat them like sons, they'll turn
out to be heroes, even if it's just in your own eyes.

WALTER SCHIRRA SR.

Father!—to God Himself, we
cannot give a holier name.

WILLIAM WORDSWORTH

You are here in order to enable the world to live
more amply, with greater vision, with a finer spirit
of hope and achievement. You are here to enrich
the world, and you impoverish yourself
if you forget the errand.

WOODROW WILSON

There is no more vital calling or
vocation for men than fathering.

JOHN THROOP

A man never stands as tall as when
he kneels to help a child.

KNIGHTS OF PYTHAGORAS

If you want your children to improve,
let them overhear the nice things you
say about them to others.

HAIM GINOTT

Good fathers make good sons.

UNKNOWN

Three things in human life are important:
The first is to be kind.
The second is to be kind.
And the third is to be kind.

HENRY JAMES

My dear brothers, take note of this: Everyone
should be quick to listen, slow to speak and slow to
become angry, for man's anger does not bring
about the righteous life that God desires.

JAMES 1:19–20 NIV

Be brave, be strong.

1 CORINTHIANS 16:13 NKJV

Feelings of worth can flourish only in an
atmosphere where individual differences are
appreciated, mistakes are tolerated, communication
is open, and rules are flexible—the kind of
atmosphere that is found in a nurturing family.

VIRGINIA SATIR

We have two ears and one mouth so that we can
listen twice as much as we speak.

EPICTETUS

There is surely something charming in
seeing the smallest thing done so thoroughly,
as if to remind the careless that whatever
is worth doing is worth doing well.

CHARLES DICKENS

For the LORD your God will bless you in all your
harvest and in all the work of your hands,
and your joy will be complete.

DEUTERONOMY 16:15 NIV

Those who trust us educate us.

GEORGE ELIOT

The most important thing a father can do for his
children is to love their mother.

THEODORE HESBURGH

He didn't tell me how to live; he lived,
and let me watch him do it.

CLARENCE BUDINGTON KELLAND

Setting an example is not the main means of influencing another, it is the only means.

ALBERT EINSTEIN

"Now that you know these things, you will be blessed if you do them."

JOHN 13:17 NIV

Live so that when your children think of fairness and integrity, they think of you.

H. JACKSON BROWN JR

Good, honest, hardheaded character is a function of the home. If the proper seed is sown there and properly nourished for a few years, it will not be easy for that plant to be uprooted.

GEORGE A. DORSEY

For you know that when your faith is tested, your endurance has a chance to grow. So let it grow, for when your endurance is fully developed, you will be perfect and complete, needing nothing.

JAMES 1:3–4 NLT

A hard worker has plenty of food,
but a person who chases
fantasies has no sense.

PROVERBS 12:11 NLT

He is rich or poor according to what he is,
not according to what he has.

HENRY WARD BEECHER

"And you shall love the LORD your God with all your
heart, with all your soul, with all your mind,
and with all your strength. This is the first
commandment."

MARK 12:30 NKJV

Act as if what you do makes a difference. It does.

WILLIAM JAMES

Make it your ambition to lead a
quiet life and attend to your own business
and work with your hands, just as we commanded
you, so that you will behave properly toward
outsiders and not be in any need.

1 THESSALONIANS 4:11–12 NASB

Responsibility is the price of greatness.

WINSTON CHURCHILL

Total Faith

A Father's Faith

Now faith is the assurance of things hoped for,
the conviction of things not seen.
HEBREWS 11:1 NASB

Faith is for those moments when nothing seems to go right. When you've reached the end of your rope and just can't hold on, and you wish you could live someone else's life—one with no troubles—you need faith.

That's because faith is tied to hope. One doesn't come without the other. When you're stuck in a tough situation, you need to be able to hold on to hope and to see the unseen long enough to know that your situation is not forever.

The author of Hebrews continues by listing many men and women and the benefits of their faith. They didn't physically receive all God's promises any more than we do, but they held on in faith, receiving many benefits in this life and an eternal reward.

Father, show me ways to strengthen my faith. My hope as a
father to my children is anchored solely in You. Amen.

The guys who fear becoming fathers
don't understand that fathering is not something
perfect men do, but something that perfects
the man. The end product of child-raising
is not the child but the parent.

FRANK PITTMAN

Many of us have inherited great riches
from our parents—the bank account
of personal faith and family prayers.

NELS F. S. FERRE

Hem your blessings with thankfulness
so they don't unravel.

UNKNOWN

Thou shalt increase my greatness,
and comfort me on every side.

PSALM 71:21 KJV

God always gives the best to those who leave the
choice with Him.

UNKNOWN

Be faithful in little things,
for in them our strength lies.

MOTHER TERESA

For God so loved the world, that he gave his only
begotten Son, that whosoever believeth in him
should not perish, but have everlasting life.

JOHN 3:16 KJV

If mountains can be moved by faith,
is there any less power in love?

FREDERICK W. FABER

All God's glory and beauty come from within, and there He delights to dwell. His visits there are frequent, His conversation sweet, His comforts refreshing, His peace passing all understanding.

THOMAS À KEMPIS

So the Lord said, "If you have faith as a mustard seed, you can say to this mulberry tree, 'Be pulled up by the roots and be planted in the sea,' and it would obey you."

LUKE 17:6 NKJV

We are so preciously loved by God that
we cannot even comprehend it. No created
being can ever know how much and how
sweetly and tenderly God loves them.

JULIAN OF NORWICH

We have boldness and access with
confidence through faith in Him.

EPHESIANS 3:12 NKJV

Of all the forces that make for a better world,
none is so indispensable, none so powerful, as hope.

CHARLES SAWYER

God showed how much he loved us by sending his one and only Son into the world so that we might have eternal life through him. This is real love—not that we loved God, but that he loved us and sent his Son as a sacrifice to take away our sins.

1 JOHN 4:9–10 NLT

The smallest bit of obedience opens heaven, and the deepest truths of God immediately become ours.

OSWALD CHAMBERS

Never talk defeat. Use words like
hope, belief, faith, victory.

NORMAN VINCENT PEALE

Fight the good fight of faith; take hold
of the eternal life to which you were called,
and you made the good confession in
the presence of many witnesses.

1 TIMOTHY 6:12 NASB

God's promises are to be the guide and measure of
our desires and expectations.

MATTHEW HENRY

Most of the important things in the world have been accomplished by people who have kept on trying when there seemed to be no hope at all.

DALE CARNEGIE

Rejoicing in hope, persevering in tribulation, devoted to prayer. . .

ROMANS 12:12 NASB

Troubles are often the tools by which God fashions us for better things.

HENRY WARD BEECHER

"For the LORD your God has blessed you in all that
you have done; He has known your wanderings
through this great wilderness. These forty years the
LORD your God has been with you;
you have not lacked a thing."

DEUTERONOMY 2:7 NASB

Truth is the beginning of every good thing,
both in heaven and on earth.

PLATO

Keep yourselves in God's love as you wait
for the mercy of our Lord Jesus Christ
to bring you to eternal life.

JUDE 1: 21 NIV

The sun. . .in its full glory, either at rising or
setting—this, and many other like blessings we
enjoy daily; and for the most of them, because they
are so common, most men forget to pay
their praises. But let not us.

IZAAK WALTON

God loves each one of us as
if there were only one of us.

AUGUSTINE

And now, dear children, remain in fellowship with
Christ so that when he returns,
you will be full of courage and not shrink
back from him in shame.

1 JOHN 2:28 NLT

Attempt great things for God;
expect great things from God.

WILLIAM CAREY

For we walk by faith, not by sight.

2 CORINTHIANS 5:7 NKJV

Trust in the Redeemer's strength. . .exercise what
faith you have, and by and by He shall rise upon you
with healing beneath His wings. Go from faith to
faith and you shall receive blessing upon blessing.

CHARLES H. SPURGEON

God is with us, and His power is around us.

CHARLES H. SPURGEON

And we know that God causes all things to work
together for good to those who love God, to those
who are called according to His purpose.

ROMANS 8:28 NASB

We were not sent into this world to do anything
into which we cannot put our hearts.

JOHN RUSKIN

The Gift of Time

A Gift for Your Children

Hear, my children, the instruction of a father, and give attention to know understanding.
PROVERBS 4:1 NKJV

One day, the nineteenth-century politician and diplomat Charles Francis Adams wrote in his personal journal, "Went fishing with my son, a day wasted." The boy, however, didn't quite see it that way. That same day, Brooks Adams wrote in his journal, "Went fishing with my father today, the most glorious day of my life!"

Many fathers are amazed when they learn, too often after the fact, what was really important to their children—namely, the meaningful time they spent enjoying Dad's company doing what otherwise might have seemed unimportant and forgettable.

We live in a busy world, one that can sap us of the time and energy it takes to spend meaningful time with those we love. Why not commit to spending at least some of your time connecting with those who are most important to you?

Father, remind me daily that You desire to use all things to help me connect meaningfully with those I love.

So much of what is great has sprung from the
closeness of family ties.

JAMES M. BARRIE

Children need love, especially
when they do not deserve it.

HAROLD HUBERT

The only rock I know that stays steady, the only
institution I know that works is the family.

LEE IACOCCA

The family: We were a strange little band of characters trying to figure out the common thread that bound us all together.

ERMA BOMBECK

Nothing you do for children is ever wasted. They seem not to notice us, hovering, averting our eyes, and they seldom offer thanks, but what we do for them is never wasted.

GARRISON KEILLOR

In bringing up children, spend on them half as much money and twice as much time.

UNKNOWN

You have a lifetime to work,
but children are only young once.

POLISH PROVERB

We find delight in the beauty and happiness of children that makes the heart too big for the body.

RALPH WALDO EMERSON

God puts each fresh morning,
each new chance of life,
into our hands as a gift to see
what we will do with it.

ANNA ROBERTSON BROWN LINDSAY

"I am with you always, even to the end of the age."

MATTHEW 28:20 NLT

The average human heart beats 100,000 times a
day. Make those beats count.

UNKNOWN

Slow down and enjoy life. It's not only the scenery you miss by going too fast—you also miss the sense of where you are going and why.

EDDIE CANTOR

Come near to God and he will come near to you.

JAMES 4:8 NIV

I have held many things in my hands and lost them all; but the things I have placed in God's hands, those I always possess.

MARTIN LUTHER

Time's a great teacher; who can live without hope?

CARL SANDBURG

And let us not be weary in well doing: for in due season we shall reap, if we faint not.

GALATIANS 6:9 KJV

I still find each day too short for all the thoughts I want to think, all the walks I want to take, all the books I want to read, and all the friends I want to see. The longer I live, the more my mind dwells upon the beauty and the wonder of the world.

JOHN BURROUGHS

Try not to become a man of success but rather try to become a man of value.

ALBERT EINSTEIN

None of the things I remember about my father had anything at all to do with his lifestyle or whom he knew or the places he had been or the style of the clothes he wore. I just knew that he was always there.

CAL THOMAS

For I am persuaded that neither death nor life,
nor angels nor principalities nor powers,
nor things present nor things to come,
nor height nor depth, nor any other created thing,
shall be able to separate us from the love of God
which is in Christ Jesus our Lord.

ROMANS 8:38–39 NKJV

The secret of happiness is not in doing what one
likes but in liking what one has to do.

JAMES M. BARRIE

Nothing is worth more than this day.

JOHANN WOLFGANG VON GOETHE

"Are not five sparrows sold for two copper coins?
And not one of them is forgotten before God.
But the very hairs of your head are all numbered.
Do not fear therefore; you are of more value
than many sparrows."

LUKE 12:6–7 NKJV

Doing little things with a strong desire to please
God makes them really great.

FRANCIS DE SALES

The fear of the LORD is the beginning of knowledge,
but fools despise wisdom and instruction.

PROVERBS 1:7 NKJV

The riches that are in the heart cannot be stolen.

RUSSIAN PROVERB

Time wasted is existence; time used is life.

EDWARD YOUNG

Let us hold fast the confession of our hope without wavering, for He who promised is faithful.

HEBREWS 10:23 NASB

Don't rob yourself the joy of this season by wishing you were in a future or past one.

CHERYL BIEHL

"I knew that you are a gracious and compassionate
God, slow to anger and abounding in love,
a God who relents from sending calamity."

JONAH 4:2 NIV

Don't put off for tomorrow what you can
do today, because if you enjoy it today,
you can do it again tomorrow.

JAMES A. MICHENER

Fill up the crevices of time with
the things that matter most.

AMY CARMICHAEL

A gentle word, a kind look, a good-natured smile
can work wonders and accomplish miracles.

WILLIAMS HAZLITT

The LORD is near to all who call upon Him,
to all who call upon Him in truth.

PSALM 145:18 NKJV

The ordinary acts we practice every day at home
are of more importance to the soul than their
simplicity might suggest.

THOMAS MOORE

A Heart for Others

Save R Sons

[From] Paul, an apostle of Christ Jesus. . .
To Timothy my true son in the faith.
1 TIMOTHY 1:1–2 NIV

In Blue Springs, Missouri, Sam is a layman burdened for boys with no male Christian influence. Through his organization "Save R Sons," his goal is to sensitize churchmen of all ages to model godly manhood for younger men who need to see it.

Sam is practicing the apostle Paul's method of "son saving." When the great missionary arrived in Lystra, he met a fatherless boy named Timothy, raised by his mother and grandmother. The two women did the best they could, but Paul could see something lacking in the young man's life. So began a series of letters, visits, and persistent prayer on the boy's behalf.

The result? Timothy became pastor of the church in Ephesus, and in Paul's last days, confidant and supporter of the apostle.

Men, if you're looking for adventure, become an example to a boy who needs what you can offer. Begin with your own family, then look for someone else's son who needs your influence.

Father, give me a heart and influence
that reaches out to others.

It is not flesh and blood but the heart
that makes us fathers and sons.

JOHANN CHRISTOPH FRIEDRICH VON SCHILLER

To be patient in little things, to be tolerant in large
affairs, to be happy in the midst of petty cares and
monotonies, that is wisdom.

JOSEPH FORT NEWTON

The memories we give may a lifetime live in the
hearts of those we hold close.

UNKNOWN

Govern a family as you would cook
a small fish—very gently.

CHINESE PROVERB

"Learn to do good; seek justice, reprove the ruthless,
defend the orphan, plead for the widow."

ISAIAH 1:17 NASB

What greater thing is there for two human souls
than to feel that they are joined for life—to be with
each other in silent unspeakable memories.

GEORGE ELIOT

By the time a man realizes that maybe
his father was right, he usually has a son
who thinks he's wrong.

CHARLES WADSWORTH

I love these little ones, and it is not a slight thing
when they, who are so fresh from God, love us.

CHARLES DICKENS

"In everything, therefore, treat people the same way
you want them to treat you, for this is the Law and
the Prophets."

MATTHEW 7:12 NASB

How far you go in life depends on your being tender with the young, compassionate with the aged, sympathetic with the striving, and tolerant of the weak and the strong. Because someday in life you will have been all of these.

GEORGE WASHINGTON CARVER

Therefore let us draw near with confidence to the throne of grace, so that we may receive mercy and find grace to help in time of need.

HEBREWS 4:16 NASB

One who is gracious to a poor man lends to the
LORD, and He will repay him for his good deed.

PROVERBS 19:17 NASB

I think I began learning long ago that those who are
happiest are those who do the most for others.

BOOKER T. WASHINGTON

Finally, all of you, live in harmony with one
another; be sympathetic, love as brothers, be
compassionate and humble.

1 PETER 3:8 NIV

There is no exercise better for the heart than
reaching down and lifting people up.

JOHN ANDREW HOLMES

Do not withhold good from those who deserve it
when it's in your power to help them. If you can
help your neighbor now, don't say, "Come back
tomorrow, and then I'll help you."

PROVERBS 3:27–28 NLT

Having someone who understands you is home.
Having someone who loves you is belonging.
Having both is a blessing.

UNKNOWN

Don't look out only for your own interests,
but take an interest in others, too.

PHILIPPIANS 2:4 NLT

Blessed are those who give without remembering.
And blessed are those who take without forgetting.

BERNARD MELTZER

For all the law is fulfilled in one word, even in this:
"You shall love your neighbor as yourself."

GALATIANS 5:14 NKJV

Forgiveness is a funny thing.
It warms the heart and cools the sting.

WILLIAM ARTHUR WARD

Each man should give what he has decided in his
heart to give, not reluctantly or under compulsion,
for God loves a cheerful giver.

2 CORINTHIANS 9:7 NIV

The first duty of love is to listen.

PAUL TILLICH

Caring is the greatest thing. Caring matters most.

FRIEDRICH VON HÜGEL

Pure and undefiled religion before God
and the Father is this: to visit orphans
and widows in their trouble, and to keep
oneself unspotted from the world.

JAMES 1:27 NKJV

To love someone means to see him
as God intended him.

FYODOR DOSTOEVSKY

The love we give away is the only love we keep.

ELBERT HUBBARD

He answereth and saith unto them, He that hath
two coats, let him impart to him that hath none;
and he that hath meat, let him do likewise.

LUKE 3:11 KJV

Carve your name on hearts and not on marble.

CHARLES H. SPURGEON

A good deed is never lost; he who sows courtesy
reaps friendship, and he who plants kindness
gathers love.

BASIL

"Give, and it will be given to you:
good measure, pressed down, shaken together,
and running over will be put into your bosom.
For with the same measure that you use,
it will be measured back to you."

LUKE 6:38 NKJV

To become truly great, one has to
stand with people, not above them.

CHARLES DE MONTESQUIEU

Therefore encourage one another and build up one
another, just as you also are doing.

1 THESSALONIANS 5:11 NASB

Throw your heart out in front of you.
And run ahead to catch it.

ARABIAN PROVERB

I want to help you grow as beautiful as God meant
for you to be when He thought of you first.

GEORGE MACDONALD

"Give generously to the poor, not gradingly. For the
LORD your God will bless you in everything you do."

DEUTERONOMY 15:10 NLT

You will find, as you look back upon your life,
that the moments when you have really lived
are the moments when you have done things
in the spirit of love.

HENRY DRUMMOND

The Joy of Kids

We're All Different

When the boys grew up, Esau was a skillful hunter, a man of the field, while Jacob was a quiet man, dwelling in tents.
GENESIS 25:27 ESV

We fathers have aspirations for our children. As they grow up, we want to pass on the things that matter most to us. For a man, that's often an interest in sports or the outdoors. But sometimes, kids just aren't wired the same way we are.

Look at Esau and Jacob. Esau was a skillful hunter. Jacob was a quiet man who preferred to dwell in a tent. Early on, their father, Isaac, favored Esau because he liked to eat the game Esau hunted.

With your own kids, look for their natural tendencies, then support them in those personal interests. Rather than choosing sides, involve yourself in your child's interests. Whether you're hunting, biking, or playing with Legos, you'll grow closer as a result.

Lord, when I'm tempted to squeeze my kids into my own mold, remind me of Jacob and Esau. Please help me to encourage my kids in their own interests.

Children are our most valuable natural resource.

HERBERT HOOVER

Children are apt to live up to what
you believe of them.

LADY BIRD JOHNSON

The most precious things of life are near at hand.

JOHN BURROUGHS

There's nothing that can help you understand your
beliefs more than trying to explain them to an
inquisitive child.

FRANK A. CLARK

Certain is it that there is no kind of affection so
purely angelic as of a father to a daughter. In love
to our wives, there is desire; to our sons, ambition;
but to our daughters, there is something which
there are no words to express.

JOSEPH ADDISON

The best portion of a good man's life is his little, nameless, unremembered acts of kindness and love.

WILLIAM WORDSWORTH

One generation plants the trees;
another gets the shade.

CHINESE PROVERB

My dear father! When I remember him, it is always with his arms open wide to love and comfort me.

ISOBEL FIELD

When I approach a child, he inspires in me two sentiments: tenderness for what he is, and respect for what he may become.

LOUIS PASTEUR

A father carries pictures where his money used to be.

UNKNOWN

It is a wise father that knows his own child.

WILLIAM SHAKESPEARE

For God has not given us a spirit of fear, but of power and of love and of a sound mind.

2 TIMOTHY 1:7 NKJV

Until you have a son of your own. . .you will never know the joy, the love beyond feeling that resonates in the heart of a father as he looks upon his son. You will never know the sense of honor that makes a man want to be more than he is and to pass something good and hopeful into the hands of his son.

KENT NERBURN

Appreciate the members of your family for who they are, even though their outlook or style may be miles different from yours. Rabbits don't fly. Eagles don't swim. Ducks look funny trying to climb. Squirrels don't have feathers. Stop comparing. There's plenty of room in the forest.

CHUCK SWINDOLL

"Therefore whoever humbles himself as this little child is the greatest in the kingdom of heaven."

MATTHEW 18:4 NKJV

Take time to laugh. It is the music of the soul.

UNKNOWN

But the Holy Spirit produces this kind of fruit
in our lives: love, joy, peace, patience, kindness,
goodness, faithfulness.

GALATIANS 5:22 NLT

Happiness is inward and not outward; and so it does
not depend on what we have, but on what we are.

HENRY VAN DYKE

Enjoy the little things, for one day you may look back and realize they were the big things.

ROBERT BRAULT

"I love those who love me; and those who diligently seek me will find me."

PROVERBS 8:17 NASB

Humor is the great thing, the saving thing. The minute it crops up, all our irritations and resentments slip away and a sunny spirit takes their place.

MARK TWAIN

Sons are a heritage from the LORD,
children a reward from him.

PSALM 127:3 NIV

Be strong and let your heart take courage,
all you who hope in the LORD.

PSALM 31:24 NASB

A young branch takes on all the
bends that one gives to it.

CHINESE PROVERB

The voyage of discovery is not in seeking new
landscapes but in having new eyes.

MARCEL PROUST

Be humble and gentle. Be patient with each other,
making allowance for each other's faults
because of your love.

EPHESIANS 4:2 NLT

The greatest use of life is to spend it
for something that will outlast it.

WILLIAM JAMES

When I was a boy of fourteen, my father
was so ignorant I could hardly stand to have
the old man around. But when I got to be twenty-
one, I was astonished at how much he
had learned in seven years.

MARK TWAIN

I can do all things through Christ
who strengthens me.

PHILIPIANS 4:13 NKJV

Let us look upon our children,
let us love them and train them,
as children of the covenant and children
of the promise—these are the children of God.

ANDREW MURRAY

A child identifies his parents with God, whether
the adults want that role or not. Most children "see"
God the way they perceive their earthly fathers.

JAMES DOBSON

Now faith is the substance of things hoped for, the
evidence of things not seen.

HEBREWS 11:1 KJV

The voice of parents is the voice of God's, for to
their children, they are heaven's lieutenants.

WILLIAM SHAKESPEARE

When we love something it is of value to us, and
when something is of value to us we spend time
with it, time enjoying it and time taking care of it.
. . . So it is when we love children; we spend time
admiring them and caring for them.
We give them our time.

M. Scott Peck

Some parents bring up their children on thunder
and lightning, but thunder and lightning never
yet made anything grow. Rain or sunshine cause
growth—quiet penetrating forces that develop life.

Unknown

True Giving

The Very Best

With my great power and outstretched arm I made the earth
and its people and the animals that are on it,
and I give it to anyone I please.
JEREMIAH 27:5 NIV

Y ou know the joy a father takes in sharing all he has, everything he can, with his kids. Fathers don't give only because they're *expected* to; they give because they want their children to have the very best.

Our heavenly Father is like that. And He demonstrated that kind of generous love when He gave us the earth and everything in it to enjoy.

The next time you're out enjoying a favorite outdoor activity—especially if you're with your children—think about how much it pleases you, an imperfect man, to give all you can to them. Then consider the perfect, giving love your heavenly Father shows you every day, in every way.

Lord, I'm amazed that You gave me everything, including the
outdoors, to enjoy—and not only that, but You were pleased
to do so!

And my God will meet all your needs according to
his glorious riches in Christ Jesus.

PHILIPPIANS 4:19 NIV

The game of life is the game of boomerangs. Our
thoughts, deeds, and words return to us sooner or
later, with astounding accuracy.

FLORENCE SCOVEL SHINN

Some people come into our lives and quickly go.
Some stay awhile and leave footprints on our
hearts, and we are never, ever the same.

UNKNOWN

The notion of responsibility is at the crux of true fatherhood. The conscious sense of responsibility for the physical and spiritual well-being of others is the mark of a true father.

CLAYTON BARBEAU

I cannot think of any need in childhood as strong as the need for a father's protection.

SIGMUND FREUD

Let parents bequeath to their children not riches, but the spirit of reverence.

PLATO

We can't give our children the future,
strive though we may to make it secure.
But we can give them the present.

KATHLEEN NORRIS

[Your children] may forget what you said, but they
will never forget how you made them feel.

CARL W. BUECHNER

Feeling gratitude and not expressing it is like
wrapping a present and not giving it.

WILLIAM ARTHUR WARD

"Being a Father" is something mythical and infinitely important: a protector, who would keep a lid on all the chaotic and catastrophic possibilities of life.

TOM WOLFE

When doubts filled my mind, your comfort gave me renewed hope and cheer.

PSALM 94:19 NLT

Have you had a kindness shown? Pass it on!

HENRY BURTON

Give thanks for unknown blessings
already on their way.

NATIVE AMERICAN PROVERB

"I have shown you in every way, by laboring like this,
that you must support the weak. And remember the
words of the Lord Jesus, that He said, 'It is more
blessed to give than to receive.'"

ACTS 20:35 NKJV

No one is useless in this world who lightens the
burdens of it for another.

CHARLES DICKENS

A kind heart is a fountain of gladness, making
everything in its vicinity freshen into smiles.

WASHINGTON IRVING

Make sure that your character is free from the love
of money, being content with what you have;
for He Himself has said, "I WILL NEVER DESERT YOU,
NOR WILL I EVER FORSAKE YOU."

HEBREWS 13:5 NASB

Give a little love to a child and you
get a great deal back.

JOHN RUSKIN

I tell you the truth, anyone who gives you a cup of water in my name because you belong to Christ will certainly not lose his reward.

MARK 9:41 NIV

A house is built of logs and stone,
of tiles and post and piers;
a home is built of loving deeds
that stand a thousand years.

VICTOR HUGO

Little children, let us not love with word or with tongue, but in deed and truth.

1 JOHN 3:18 NASB

It is well with the man who is gracious and lends; he will maintain his cause in judgment.

PSALM 112:5 NASB

To give without any reward, or any notice, has a special quality of its own.

ANNE MORROW LINDBERGH

There never was any heart truly great and generous, that was not also tender and compassionate.

ROBERT SOUTH

"Give, and you will receive. Your gift will return to you in full—pressed down, shaken together to make room for more, running over, and poured into your lap. The amount you give will determine the amount you get back."

LUKE 6:38 NLT

Happiness is like perfume; you can't
pour it on someone else without getting
a few drops on yourself.

JAMES VAN DER ZEE

Every good gift and every perfect gift is from
above, and comes down from the Father of lights,
with whom there is no variation or shadow of
turning. Of His own will He brought us forth
by the word of truth, that we might be a kind
of firstfruits of His creatures.

JAMES 1:17–18 NKJV

Thus speaketh the LORD of hosts, saying, Execute true judgment, and shew mercy and compassions every man to his brother.

ZECHARIAH 7:9 KJV

If God gives you the wonderful gift of children, don't let a day go by without pronouncing God's blessing over their lives. This is a spiritual right and responsibility of fathers.

DAVID SHIBLEY

Rest

Song of the Stars

Praise him, sun and moon, praise him,
all you shining stars.
PSALM 148:3 NIV

When was the last time you stood alone in the night, watching the stars?

God's handiwork can be millions of miles away— yet as close as a quiet moment in the backyard. Did you ever stop to think that you are seeing the same stars that shone on King David, Christopher Columbus, and George Washington? Those stars were placed on the day God created the heavens—and still point us to our powerful Lord today.

So many of us are caught up in the rat race, searching for peace but missing some of the quiet signposts to God's presence. The night sky holds a million secrets—and waits for us to step away from this hectic world and reach for His hand.

If your life seems to be careening out of control, stop the treadmill. Pull the power cord of your existence for a while, and listen to the song of the stars. Your Creator waits on you, tonight.

Gracious God, my Creator, please help me
to stop racing long enough to hear Your voice
when I gaze in wonder at the stars.

Can't you see the Creator of the universe, who understands every secret, every mystery, sitting patiently and listening to a four-year-old talk to Him? That's a beautiful image of a father.

JAMES DOBSON

[Cast] all your care upon Him,
for He cares for you.

1 PETER 5:7 NKJV

True silence is the rest of the mind; it is to the spirit what sleep is to the body, nourishment and refreshment.

WILLIAM PENN

Let us not hurry so in our pace of living that we
lose sight of the art of living.

SIR FRANCIS BACON

The LORD is my strength and my shield; my heart
trusted in Him, and I am helped; therefore my heart
greatly rejoices, and with my song I will praise Him.

PSALM 28:7 NKJV

As we. . .thrive on simple pleasures, our work,
our families, our entire lives can be renewed.

UNKNOWN

Rest is not idleness, and to lie sometimes on the grass under the trees on a summer's day, listening to the murmur of water or watching the clouds float across the sky, is by no means a waste of time.

JOHN LUBBOCK

Like a shepherd He will tend His flock, in His arm He will gather the lambs and carry them in His bosom; He will gently lead the nursing ewes.

ISAIAH 40:11 NASB

Rest when you're weary. Refresh and renew
yourself, your body, your mind, your spirit.
Then get back to work.

RALPH MARSTON

There shall be no night there: They need no lamp
nor light of the sun, for the Lord God gives them
light. And they shall reign forever and ever.

REVELATION 22:5 NKJV

"You will go out in joy and be led forth in peace; the mountains and hills will burst into song before you, and all the trees of the field will clap their hands."

Isaiah 55:12 NIV

The time to relax is when you don't have time for it.

Sydney J. Harris

If people concentrated on the really important things in life, there'd be a shortage of fishing poles.

DOUG LARSON

The LORD is good, a stronghold in the day of trouble; and He knows those who trust in Him.

NAHUM 1:7 NKJV

Tension is who you think you should be. Relaxation is who you are.

CHINESE PROVERB

Peace is not something you wish for; it's something you make, something you do, something you are, and something you give away.

ROBERT FULGHUM

"Rejoice in that day and leap for joy! For indeed your reward is great in heaven, for in like manner their fathers did to the prophets."

LUKE 6:23 NKJV

When you find peace within yourself, you become the kind of person who can live at peace with others.

PEACE PILGRIM

Do not let trifles disturb your tranquility of mind. . . .
Life is too precious to be sacrificed
for the nonessential and transient. . . .
Ignore the inconsequential.

GRENVILLE KLEISER

As for God, His way is blameless;
the word of the LORD is tried;
He is a shield to all who take refuge in Him.

PSALM 18:30 NASB

How beautiful it is to do nothing,
and then to rest afterward.

SPANISH PROVERB

A cheerful heart is good medicine, but a crushed
spirit dries up the bones.

PROVERBS 17:22 NIV

Every now and then go away, have a little
relaxation, for when you come back to your work
your judgment will be surer. Go some distance away
because then the work appears smaller and more of
it can be taken in at a glance and a lack of harmony
and proportion is more readily seen.

LEONARDO DA VINCI

"Come to Me, all you who labor and are heavy
laden, and I will give you rest. Take My yoke upon
you and learn from Me, for I am gentle and lowly in
heart, and you will find rest for your souls. For My
yoke is easy and My burden is light."

MATTHEW 11:28–30 NKJV

Take rest; a field that has rested
gives a bountiful crop.

OVID

Sometimes it's important to work for that pot of gold. But other times it's essential to take time off and to make sure that your most important decision in the day simply consists of choosing which color to slide down on the rainbow.

DOUGLAS PAGELS

"Six days you shall labor and do all your work, but the seventh day is the Sabbath of the LORD your God. In it you shall do no work: you, nor your son, nor your daughter, nor your male servant, nor your female servant, nor your cattle, nor your stranger who is within your gates."

EXODUS 20:9–10 NKJV

He that can take rest is greater than
he that can take cities.

BENJAMIN FRANKLIN

The things which you learned and received and
heard and saw in me, these do, and the God of
peace will be with you.

PHILIPPIANS 4:9 NKJV

Half our life is spent trying to find something
to do with the time we have rushed through
life trying to save.

WILL ROGERS

It's important to be heroic, ambitious, productive,
efficient, creative, and progressive, but these
qualities don't necessarily nurture the soul.
The soul has different concerns, of equal value:
downtime for reflection, conversation, and
reverie; beauty that is captivating and pleasuring;
relatedness to the environs and to people; and any
animal's rhythm of rest and activity.

THOMAS MOORE

Peace I leave with you, my peace I give unto you: not
as the world giveth, give I unto you. Let not your
heart be troubled, neither let it be afraid.

JOHN 14:27 KJV

Dad = Fun

A Day in the Park

So do not fear, for I am with you; do not be dismayed,
for I am your God. I will strengthen you and help you; I
will uphold you with my righteous right hand.
ISAIAH 41:10 NIV

On a sunny day in the park, a father held his young son upside down. The boy squealed and laughed with delight as his daddy swung him by the ankles, back and forth over the ground. It never occurred to the child that he could possibly be dropped on his head!

Children often express total faith in their parents, believing that as long as they're in their father's hands, they'll be safe. Kids will enjoy their dad's hair-raising "airplane rides" without the least hesitation. As the boy in the park yelled, when his father finally lowered him safely to the ground, "Again! Again!"

Imagine how much more we could enjoy our lives if we could simply realize that we are in our heavenly Father's hands. There should be no fear of any accidental drops, as long as our Lord has us in His grip. Our Father holds us securely. . .and He will not let us fall.

Lord, forgive me for sometimes forgetting that I am in
Your safe and loving hands.

A happy family is but an earlier heaven.

GEORGE BERNARD SHAW

We never know the love of our parents
for us till we have become parents.

HENRY WARD BEECHER

Sacred and happy homes are the surest guarantees
for the moral progress of a nation.

HENRY DRUMMOND

My father gave me the greatest gift anyone could
give another person—he believed in me.

JIM VALVANO

Fatherhood is pretending the present
you love most is soap-on-a-rope.

BILL COSBY

My father used to play with my brother and me in
the yard. Mother would come out and say, "You're
tearing up the grass." "We're not raising grass," Dad
would reply. "We're raising boys."

HARMON KILLEBREW

Believe that life is worth living,
and your belief will help create the fact.

WILLIAM JAMES

I will praise You, O LORD, with my whole heart;
I will tell of all Your marvelous works.

PSALM 9:1 NKJV

Always laugh when you can; it is cheap medicine.
Merriment. . .is the sunny side of existence.

LORD BYRON

"But from there you will seek the LORD your
God, and you will find Him if you seek Him with
all your heart and with all your soul."

DEUTERONOMY 4:29 NKJV

Whether sixty or sixteen, there is in every
human being's heart the love of wonder,
the sweet amazement at the stars and starlike
things, the undaunted challenge of events,
the unfailing childlike appetite for what-next,
and the joy of the game of living.

SAMUEL ULLMAN

If a child is to keep alive his inborn sense of wonder, he needs the companionship of at least one adult who can share it, rediscovering with him the joy, excitement, and mystery of the world we live in.

RACHEL CARSON

But as many as received Him, to them He gave the right to become children of God, even to those who believe in His name.

JOHN 1:12 NASB

If one advances confidently in the direction of his dreams and endeavors to live the life which he has imagined, he will meet with a success unexpected in common hours. Go confidently in the direction of your dreams! Live the life you've imagined!

HENRY DAVID THOREAU

Keep yourselves in God's love as you wait for the mercy of our Lord Jesus Christ to bring you to eternal life.

JUDE 1:21 NIV

One of the best parts of being a dad is that it means you never really have to grow up all the way. You can still rough house and goof around and act foolish; in fact, the more you do it, the more your kids giggle. What a great deal: You get to show off like a ten-year-old, *and* you have a nonstop, appreciative audience for every silly thing you do.

BEN PRESTON

Dads are stone skimmers, mud wallowers, water wallopers, ceiling swoopers, shoulder gallopers, upsy-downsy, over-and-through, round-and-about whoosers. Dads are smugglers and secret sharers.

HELEN THOMSON

The real joy of life is in its play. Play is anything we do for the joy and love of doing it, apart from any profit, compulsion, or sense of duty.
It is the real living of life.

WALTER RAUSCHENBUSCH

And whatever you do or say, do it as a representative of the Lord Jesus, giving thanks through him to God the Father.

COLOSSIANS 3:17 NLT

Doubly rich is the man still boyish enough to play, laugh and sing as he carries and emanates sunshine along a friendly road.

CHARLES R. WIERS

The great man is he who does
not lose his child's heart.

MENCIUS

There are three stages of a man's life: He believes in
Santa Claus, he doesn't believe in Santa Claus,
he is Santa Claus.

UNKNOWN

Up on his shoulders. . .is where I love to be.

MICHAEL CARR

The essence of childhood, of course, is play, which
my friends and I did endlessly on streets that we
reluctantly shared with traffic.

BILL COSBY

Thou wilt keep him in perfect peace, whose mind is
stayed on thee: because he trusteth in thee.

ISAIAH 26:3 KJV

Our whole life is but a greater
and longer childhood.

BENJAMIN FRANKLIN

Glory to the Father give,
God in whom we move and live;
Children's prayers He deigns to hear,
Children's songs delight His ear.

JAMES MONTGOMERY

To show a child what once delighted you,
to find the child's delight added to your own—
this is happiness.

J. B. PRIESTLY

We don't stop playing because we grow old;
we grow old because we stop playing.

GEORGE BERNARD SHAW

Each day of our lives, we make deposits in the
memory banks of our children.

CHARLES R. SWINDOLL

Sometimes the grace of god appears
wonderfully in young children.

MATTHEW HENRY

There are not seven wonders of the world in the eyes of a child. There are seven million.

WALT STREIGHTIFF

If I had a child to raise all over again, I'd build self-esteem first and the house later. I'd fingerpaint more and point the finger less. I would do less correcting and more connecting. I'd take my eyes off my watch, and watch with my eyes. I'd take more hikes and fly more kites. I'd stop playing serious and seriously play. I would run through more fields and gaze at more stars. I'd do more hugging and less tugging.

DIANE LOOMANS

The Value of Family

Sharing God's Peace

All your children shall be taught by the LORD,
and great shall be the peace of your children.
ISAIAH 54:13 NKJV

W e can prepare our children for life on their own, but the best thing we can do for them is to introduce them to the Lord. He is the only One who can give them peace.

What is the greatest hope you have for your family? Isn't it that, no matter what they become or accomplish, they will be happy? How can you teach them that? Your children may be rich or poor, famous or humble, but only God's peace will bring them true happiness.

Father, only You and Your lessons can give our children the happiness we want for them. We do the best we can for them and trust the rest to You.

There should be peace at home.

ISAAC WATTS

The love of a family is life's greatest blessing.

UNKNOWN

Praise the children and they will blossom.

IRISH PROVERB

It's difficult to imagine anything more nourishing
to the soul than family life.

THOMAS MOORE

"I have told you all this so that you may have peace
in me. Here on earth you will have many trials and
sorrows. But take heart, because I have overcome
the world."

JOHN 16:33 NLT

Perhaps the greatest social service that can be
rendered by anybody to the country and
to mankind is to bring up a family.

GEORGE BERNARD SHAW

Family ties are bound by love.

UNKNOWN

He that raises a large family does, indeed, while
he lives to observe them, stand a broader mark for
sorrow; but then he stands a broader mark
for pleasure, too.

BENJAMIN FRANKLIN

Parents must respect the spiritual person of their child and approach it with reverence.

GEORGE MACDONALD

Someday you will know that a father is much happier in his children's happiness than in his own. I cannot explain it to you: It is a feeling in your body that spreads gladness through you.

HONORÉ DE BALZAC

The love of a family is life's greatest blessing.

UNKNOWN

The family is the nucleus of civilization.

WILLIAM J. DURANT

Love and fear: Everything the father of a family
says must inspire one or the other.

JOSEPH JOUBERT

He loveth righteousness and judgment: the earth is
full of the goodness of the LORD.

PSALM 33:5 KJV

The Christian home is the Master's workshop where the processes of character-molding are silently, lovingly, faithfully, and successfully carried on.

RICHARD MONCKTON MILNES

Be perfect, be of good comfort, be of one mind, live in peace; and the God of love and peace shall be with you.

2 CORINTHIANS 13:11 KJV

So much of what is great has sprung from the closeness of family ties.

JAMES M. BARRIE

No legacy is so rich as honesty.

WILLIAM SHAKESPEARE

Where we love is home, home that our feet may
leave, but not our hearts.

OLIVER WENDELL HOLMES

What greater thing is there for human souls than to feel that they are joined for life—to be with each other in silent unspeakable memories.

GEORGE ELIOT

Trust in the LORD with all your heart, and lean not on your own understanding.

PROVERBS 3:5 NKJV

Mid pleasures and palaces though we may roam, be it ever so humble, there's no place like home.

JOHN HOWARD PAYNE

Life's lasting joy comes in erasing the boundary
between "mine" and "yours."

UNKNOWN

All your children shall be taught by the LORD, and
great shall be the peace of your children.

ISAIAH 54:13 NKJV

A man travels the world over in search of what he
needs and returns home to find it.

GEORGE MOORE

Behold what manner of love the
Father has bestowed on us, that we
should be called children of God!

1 JOHN 3:1 NKJV

For the Scriptures say, "If you want to enjoy life and
see many happy days, keep your tongue from speaking
evil and keep your lips from telling lies. Turn away
from evil and do good. Search for peace,
and work to maintain it."

1 PETER 3:10–11 NLT

Favorite people, favorite places,
favorite memories of the past—
These are the joys of a lifetime;
these are the things that last.

HENRY VAN DYKE

For it is You who blesses the righteous man, O
LORD, You surround him with favor as with a shield.

PSALM 5:12 NASB

The happiest moments of my life have been
the few which I have passed at home in
the bosom of my family.

THOMAS JEFFERSON

A good laugh is sunshine in a house.

WILLIAM MAKEPEACE THACKERAY

For you are all sons of God through
faith in Christ Jesus.

GALATIANS 3:26 NKJV

Happy will that house be in which relations are
formed from character.

RALPH WALDO EMERSON

Family relationships are the purest, cleanest, whitest sand of all.

ROBERT H. BENSON

"Those who accept my commandments and obey them are the ones who love me. And because they love me, my Father will love them. And I will love them and reveal myself to each of them."

JOHN 14:21 NLT

Love begins by taking care of the closest ones—the ones at home.

MOTHER TERESA

Dad = Teacher

A Positive Example

"Teach them the decrees and laws, and show them the way to live and the duties they are to perform."
EXODUS 18:20 NIV

Working parents and stay-at-home moms and dads agree: We don't have enough time with our children. It's only natural that when we are with them, we want those hours to be filled with fun and not lectures. Yet it is the duty of parents to be teachers and not best buddies, and we are not doing right by our children unless we teach them how to live in a godly manner.

Who else is going to teach them manners? Who else cares as much about their honesty and decency?

Instead of lectures, though, we should strive to give them constant positive examples. Through your own life you will teach them what you value. If you want Christian children, you must live as a Christian father.

Father, bringing up children is the parents' job, and not one for society. When I am being a bad example, show me my error. Be my teacher so I can teach my children how to live in faith.

When I was a boy of fourteen,
my father was so ignorant I could hardly
stand to have the old man around. But when
I got to be twenty-one, I was astonished at how
much he had learned in seven years.

MARK TWAIN

Parents can only give good advice or put them on
the right paths, but the final forming of a person's
character lies in their own hands.

ANNE FRANK

Hate evil, love good,
and establish justice in the gate!

AMOS 5:15 NASB

I talk and talk and talk, and I haven't taught people
in fifty years what my father taught by example
in one week.

MARIO CUOMO

The only thing to do with good advice is pass it on.
It is never any use to oneself.

OSCAR WILDE

Before I got married, I had six theories about
bringing up children; now I have six children
and no theories.

JOHN WILMOT

He who teaches children learns more than they do.

GERMAN PROVERB

Kids learn by example. If I respect Mom,
they're going to respect Mom.

TIM ALLEN

There are two great injustices that can befall a
child. One is to punish him for something he didn't
do. The other is to let him get away with doing
something he knows is wrong.

ROBERT GARDNER

Don't be discouraged if your children
reject your advice. Years later, they will
offer it to their own offspring.

UNKNOWN

Let no corrupt word proceed out of your mouth,
but what is good for necessary edification,
that it may impart grace to the hearers.

EPHESIANS 4:29 NKJV

The most important work you and I will ever do will
be within the walls of our own homes.

HAROLD B. LEE

Noble fathers have noble children.

EURIPIDES

A good father reflects the love
of the heavenly Father.

UNKNOWN

He who keeps instruction is in the way of life,
but he who refuses correction goes astray.

PROVERBS 10:17 NKJV

Character is largely caught, and the father and the
home should be the great sources of
character infection.

FRANK H. CHELEY

If you want children to keep their feet on the
ground, put some responsibility on their shoulders.

ABIGAIL VAN BUREN

Don't worry that children never listen to you;
worry that they are always watching you.

ROBERT FULGHUM

He that gives good advice, builds with
one hand; he that gives good counsel and
example, builds with both; but he that gives
good admonition and bad example, builds with
one hand and pulls down with the other.

FRANCIS BACON SR.

My dear father, my dear friend, the best and wisest
man I ever knew, who taught me many lessons and
showed me many things as we went together along
the country byways.

SARAH ORNE JEWETT

One father is more than a hundred schoolmasters.

Geoge Herbert

In the final analysis, it is not what you do for
your children but what you have taught them
to do for themselves that will make them
successful human beings.

Ann Landers

Listen to counsel and accept discipline,
that you may be wise the rest of your days.

Proverbs 19:20 nasb

Every father should remember that one day his son
will follow his example instead of his advice.

UNKNOWN

Control your temper,
for anger labels you a fool.

ECCLESIASTES 7:9 NLT

To make mistakes is human;
to stumble is commonplace;
to be able to laugh at yourself is maturity.

WILLIAM ARTHUR WARD

The world is not a playground; it is a schoolroom.
Life is not a holiday, but an education. And the one
eternal lesson for us all is how better we can love.

HENRY DRUMMOND

Obey your leaders and submit to their authority. They
keep watch over you as men who must give an account.
Obey them so that their work will be a joy, not a
burden, for that would be of no advantage to you.

HEBREWS 13:17 NIV

If there is righteousness in the heart, there will be beauty in the character. If there is beauty in the character, if there is harmony in the home, there will be order in the nation.

CHINESE PROVERB

My son, do not forget my teaching, but keep my commands in your heart, for they will prolong your life many years and bring you prosperity.

PROVERBS 3:1–2 NIV